Primarily MATH

• A Problem Solving Approach •

Written by Sharon Eckert and Judy Leimbach

Illustrated by Annelise Palouda
Cover by Elisa Ahlin

Published by Prufrock Press Inc.

Copyright ©2005 Prufrock Press Inc.

Printed in the United States of America.

ISBN-13: 978-1-59363-123-9
ISBN-10: 1-59363-123-5

Prufrock Press, Inc.
P.O. Box 8813
Waco, Texas 76714-8813
(800) 998-2208
Fax (800) 240-0333
http://www.prufrock.com

Contents

Notes

Information for the Instructor

Why teach problem solving?

"Problem solving should be the central focus of the mathematics curriculum. As such, it is a primary goal of all mathematics instruction and an integral part of all mathematical activity."

This quote comes from the document *Curriculum and Evaluation Standards for School Mathematics* issued by the National Council of Teachers of Mathematics. Generally referred to as the NCTM standards, these guidelines were written in response to inadequate mathematical preparation in our schools in grades kindergarten through 12th grade. The NCTM standards set forth broad goals for students. These are:

1. that students learn to value mathematics,
2. that students become confident in their ability to do mathematics,
3. that students become mathematical problem solvers,
4. that students learn to communicate mathematically, and
5. that students learn to reason mathematically.

According to the NCTM standards, "Problem solving is not a distinct topic, but a process that should permeate the entire program and provide the context in which concepts and skills can be learned."

It is important, therefore, that schools emphasize a problem-solving approach to mathematics beginning in the early years and continuing through high school. Students should learn to value the process of solving problems as well as getting the correct solutions. This can be done by:

- teaching students a variety of strategies to solve mathematical problems,

- giving them opportunities to experience different ways of solving problems,

- stressing that different approaches and strategies can be used to solve a particular problem, and

- allowing them to share their thinking about how they solved the problem.

The strategies in this book will help students reason, develop their problem-solving strategies, grow in their ability to communicate mathematically, and develop confidence in their mathematical abilities.

What problem-solving strategies should you teach?

If you consulted the various resources on mathematical problem solving, you would find that there are many different lists of problem-solving strategies. A program incorporating all of the strategies would be overwhelming for primary students. Therefore, we have grouped related strategies together and have chosen to concentrate on just five problem solving strategies that are most appropriate for primary grade students. The strategies that will be presented in this book are:

1. draw a picture or diagram
2. use manipulatives or act out
3. extend a repeating pattern
4. make a table, list or chart
5. choose relevant information

Some of the other strategies, such as guessing and checking and reasoning logically, will be used along with the five areas we have chosen to concentrate on in this book.

What kind of classroom climate is conducive to problem solving?

A climate that is conducive to problem solving is as important as the problems you use in your math problem and should be your primary goal. The classroom climate is a combination of the teacher's attitudes and actions, the way students are grouped, how students are evaluated, and the content and instruction that are presented. Varying these elements produces either a climate in which students feel comfortable with playing around with numbers, problems and solutions or a climate in which students learn to perform rote procedures and throw up their hands in despair when problems differ from the standard format.

In order to develop into successful problem solvers, it is important that students feel free to experiment, think, talk about their thinking, and make mistakes. Problem-solving behavior will not flourish in an environment that stresses doing the problem by yourself, getting the right answer, or doing the problem just the way the instructor has presented it. Instead, we need to encourage students to be open-minded, to be curious, to explore, to try different things and to make guesses. When these characteristics are valued and encouraged, problem-solving behavior will flourish. These are some of the things you can do to encourage this kind of behavior:

- Let students know that it is okay to be puzzled by a problem.

- Allow lots of time for students to work on a problem.

- Encourage experimentation — trying different strategies to find one that works.

- Encourage students to work together and share their ideas.

- Encourage students to talk about the way they solved the problem.

- Create a relaxed, comfortable environment.

- Encourage a creative approach rather than following a lock-step routine.

How do you introduce problem solving?

Students need to be introduced to problem solving strategies before they can be expected to use these strategies on their own. The most effective approach is to introduce each strategy in a whole-class lesson where you not only present the problem but you use questioning to guide students to successful completion of the problem. This approach should be followed by a couple of other lessons when the problem is presented to the whole class and either the class works it together under your guidance or in small groups, trying different approaches and discussing their thinking.

The first few times you present problems that students are to solve by themselves or with partners, you may wish to indicate which strategy would be the most appropriate to use. After the first few independent sessions, you should not indicate how students are to approach the problems. It is better at this point that they experiment with different strategies to find the one that works best. In most cases, there will be more than one way to solve the problem.

What are the stages of problem solving?

There are four different stages that students will need to progress through as they attempt to solve a problem. These stages are:

1. Understanding the problem

At this stage students need to read the problem, clarify any words or concepts that they don't understand, and find the important information. You should ask your students questions that will help them understand the problem and ask them to state what they think they are supposed to find out.

2. Devising a plan

At this point students should consider how they will solve the problem. Since they can reach the same answer in various ways, they should consider a couple of different approaches. Your questioning can reinforce groups who have chosen appropriate strategies and redirect students who are having difficulty selecting a strategy that will be productive.

3. Solving the problem

Here the students do the actual calculations or manipulations and arrive at an answer. Encourage students to talk about what they are doing and why they think their procedure is a valid one.

4. Checking the problem

At this point students should check their answer to make sure it makes sense. They should also check the arithmetic to make sure it was done correctly. Discuss the problem and how it was solved. What worked and what didn't work? Talk about related or extended problems. Ask students to suggest real-life problems that are similar.

How do you use this book?

This book is organized into six sections. The first five sections teach the problem-solving strategies listed above, and the last section presents a variety of problems so students can apply the skills they learned in the first five sections.

Sections 1-5 are organized in the following way: .

* **Teacher's Introduction** - This section introduces the strategy, explains how to solve the introductory and practice problems, and provides the answers to these problems.

* **Introductory Lessons** - These lessons are to be teacher-directed but are interactive, enabling students to learn the strategies by doing them.

* **Practice Problems** - These pages provide guided practice in each strategy. They are intended to be used for individual or paired practice. Input from the instructor should be in the form of questions that guide students' thinking and problem solving.

Section 6

The last section provides practice in applying the various strategies. It presents a variety of problems that will give students the opportunity to apply the problem solving strategies they have learned in the first five sections of the book. The pages are not grouped in any way and can be used in any order. A particular strategy has not been designated for these pages. Instead, emphasis should be placed on the fact that several strategies can be used successfully with any given problem.

Do your students need extra challenge?

Because most students in the primary grades are just learning problem-solving strategies, the problems in this book have been kept relatively straightforward and ask for only a single answer. Many of the problems, however, could be the basis for additional problems. If your students are ready to tackle multifaceted problems, you might consider adding other questions, posing the questions either in writing by adding to the problem or orally when students are discussing their work.

Here are a few examples of questions you might want to pose to extend the problems as given.

Make a Table - Practice Problem 8 (page 53)

* *How many seating combinations allowed Ann to sit in the middle?*

* *How many seating combinations allowed Ann and Heidi to be seated next to each other?*

Application - Problem 5 (page 66)

* *How many times did Rita's mother drive on Tuesdays?*

Application - Problem 23 (page 75)

* *Who had the fewest turns?*

* *Who watered the plants during the 8th week?*

* *How many weeks did Karen water the plants?*

Application - Problem 35 (page 81)

* *How many red squares will be along the left side of the quilt when it is finished?*

* *How many blue squares will there be in the quilt?*

Application - problem 38 (page 82)

* *What color would the last row start with?*

* *What color would be in the center of the garden?*

Application - Problem 40 (page 83)

* *If three people changed their minds at 1:50 p.m. and went home, how many people would be in line at that time?*

Application - Problem 46 (page 86)

* *What day of the week had the most even numbered days when she could water?*

Using Manipulatives or Acting Out

This strategy involves using concrete objects to represent the information given in a problem. Using this strategy, students are able to act out the problem and actually "see" the solution.

Performing the operations with manipulatives and acting out the processes are the basis for understanding symbolism in math. Before we ask students to do computation using mathematical symbols, we need to provide them with concrete experiences that will help them internalize the meaning of those symbols. Young students need opportunities to try to find solutions by maneuvering the objects until they fit the conditions outlined in the problem. Some problems appear quite complicated or confusing. Often this is because they have a number of steps to them. However, the problems become simplified and easy to follow when they are acted out. When students successfully solve these complex problems they develop a positive attitude toward math and build confidence in their own abilities as problem solvers.

This section presents a variety of problems that lend themselves to an individual student using unifix cubes or other manipulatives to find the solution. Also included are problems that lend themselves to having a group of students actually act out the problem. For these problems, we suggest using name tags to label the students, showing who or what they represent.

Instructional Notes

Introductory Lesson 1

To solve this problem, use manipulatives to represent the pieces of candy. Put Judy's 13 pieces in one line and Tom's 3 pieces in another. Then move pieces of candy from Judy's line to Tom's line until the two lines are equal.

Answer: 5 pieces

Introductory Lessons 2 - 4

Introductory problems 2, 3, and 4 are solved in a fashion similar to the problem above.

Lesson 2

Answer: 5 pennies

Lesson 3

Answer: 11 stickers

Lesson 4

Answer: Carla - 1 pencil   Shawn - 4 pencils

Introductory Lesson 5

One good way to solve this problem is to act it out. Use index cards or other manipulatives to represent the baseball cards. Have three people wear name tags to represent Lisa, Byron and Megan. Give each person 10 cards. Have them perform the actions that are indicated in the problem. For instance, for the first set of instructions, have Lisa give Byron 4 cards and Megan 3 cards. Continue in the same manner until the trading is completed.

Answer: Lisa - 10; Byron - 7; Megan - 13

Introductory Lesson 6

In this problem students will have to place five objects on the table for each pack of gum, making a total of 20 objects. They can then divide the objects into five equal groups. Once they know that each person will end up with 4 sticks of gum, and they know that Linda started out with 5 pieces and Rob with 15 pieces, they can figure out how many pieces of gum each will have to give away.

Answer: Linda gives away 1 stick of gum.
   Rob gives away 11 pieces of gum (2 packs and 1 stick).
   Each person will then have 4 pieces of gum.

Practice Lesson 7

Students should start with 29 items and add or take away objects to represent people boarding or leaving the train.

Answer: 25 passengers

Practice Lesson 8

Students should lay down 10 objects and then 8 objects. They can then start arranging the objects into 3 even rows.

Answer: 6 on each shelf

Practice Lesson 9

Students should begin with 18 objects. They can then divide them into two groups - a purple group and a yellow group. For every object they put in the purple pile, they should put two objects in the yellow pile.

Answer: 12 yellow, 6 purple

Practice Lesson 10

This is a multi-stage problem. First students will have to establish that Kristin has 8 balloons, Kurt has 14 balloons, and Kyle has 5 balloons. They can then move around objects until all three people have 9 balloons each.

Answer: Kurt gives Kristin 1 balloon.
   Kurt gives Kyle 4 balloons.

Name _____

Trading Candy

Judy had 13 pieces of candy. Tom had 3 pieces of candy. How many pieces did Judy give Tom so that they both had the same number of pieces?

Judy gave Tom _____ pieces of candy.

Name _____

Penny Swap

Juanita had 6 pennies and Terrell had 16 pennies. How many pennies did Terrell give Juanita so that they both had the same number of pennies?

Terrell gave Juanita _____ pennies.

Name _____

Sharing Stickers

Janis had 9 stickers and Adam had 31 stickers. How many stickers did Adam give Janis so that they both had the same number of stickers?

Adam gave Janis _____ stickers.

Name _____

Pencils, Please

Heather had 15 pencils, Carla had 9 pencils and Shawn had 6 pencils. How many pencils did Heather give Carla and Shawn so that they all had the same number of pencils?

Heather gave Carla _____ pencils.

Heather gave Shawn _____ pencils.

Name _____

Trading Baseball Cards

Lisa, Byron and Megan each had 10 baseball cards before they began trading cards. Lisa gave 4 of her cards to Byron and 3 to Megan. Byron gave 6 of his cards to Megan and 5 to Lisa. Megan gave 2 of her cards to Lisa and 4 to Byron. How many cards did each child have after they were done trading?

Lisa had _____ cards.

Byron had _____ cards.

Megan had _____ cards.

Name _____

Yummy Gummy

Linda has 1 pack of gum. Rob has 3 packs of gum. Each pack has 5 pieces of gum in it. They want to share the gum with 3 other friends so all 5 people have the same number of sticks. How can they do this?

Linda gives away _____ sticks of gum.

Rob gives away _____ sticks of gum.

Each person will then have _____ sticks of gum.

Name _____

Train Ride

A train left the station with 29 passengers. At the first stop 5 people got off and 6 got on. At the second stop 12 people got off and 7 got on. How many people were on the train when it pulled away from the second stop?

There were _____ people on the train.

Name _____

Stuffed Animal Collections

Amber and Kevin collected stuffed animals. Amber had 10 animals and Kevin had 8.
They displayed their animals together on three shelves with the same number of
animals on each shelf. How many animals were on each shelf?

There were _____ animals on each shelf.

© Prufrock Press Inc • *Primarily Math*

Name _____

Jose's Marbles

Jose has 18 yellow and purple marbles. He has twice as many yellow marbles as purple ones. How many marbles of each color does Jose have?

Jose has _____ yellow marbles and _____ purple marbles.

Name _____

Friends with Balloons

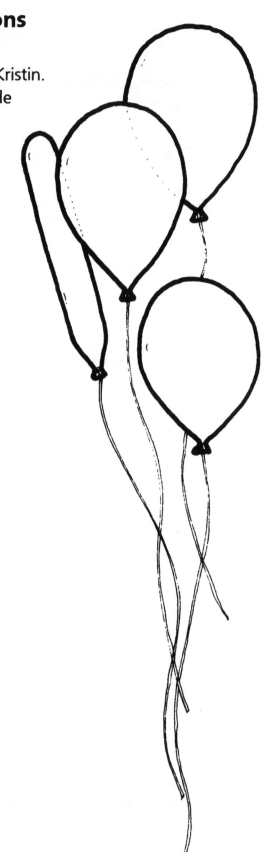

Kristin has 8 balloons. Kurt has 6 more balloons than Kristin. Kyle has 3 less balloons than Kristin. They want to trade balloons so they all have the same number. How can they do this?

Kurt gives Kristin _____ balloons.

Kurt gives Kyle _____ balloons.

Draw a Picture or Diagram

The strategy of drawing a picture or a diagram to represent the information in a problem involves more abstract thinking than using manipulatives and acting out, but it still gives students something to help them "see" and understand the problem.

Constructing a picture or diagram for themselves helps students clarify the problem in their own minds. Looking at a picture or diagram in their math book can be helpful for some children; however, actually drawing their own picture is important because it requires them to think through the problem and decide how to depict the information so as to lead to a solution. Students may draw their pictures or diagrams in different ways. Some students may progress to the stage where they can visualize the picture in their mind without needing to draw it on paper.

This chapter presents some seemingly complex problems that become quite simple when the strategy of making a picture or diagram is applied.

Instructional Notes

Introductory Lesson 1

To solve this problem, students should draw a picture. First they should draw 8 circles to represent the 8 pets. Since you know that all of her pets have at least two legs, you can then draw two legs on each pet. At this point, ask students how many legs they have drawn (16). Suggest that since that is less than the total number of legs mentioned in the problem (24) that they need to draw more legs. Since no animal has 3 legs, they need to continue to draw 2 more legs on some of the pets until there are a total of 24 legs. The circles with only 2 legs represent the birds.

Answer: 4 birds

Introductory Lesson 2

Have students start by drawing circles to represent the total number of pets as they did with the first problem. They should continue by drawing two legs on all of the circles and then adding two more legs to each circle until they get a total of 16 legs.

Answer: 2 hamsters

Introductory Lesson 3

Students should begin by drawing 25 lines to represent the 25 children in line. Then they should continue by dividing them into groups of 3 until they have 6 groups of 3. The remaining lines will be the number of children still waiting for a ride.

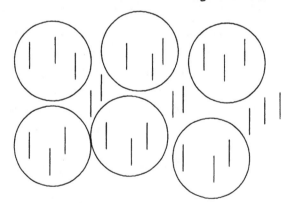

Answer: 7 children

Introductory Lesson 4

Students should draw 8 chairs and then draw 3 people in each chair until they have drawn 10 people. They can then count the remaining spaces.

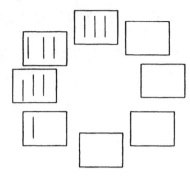

Answer: 14 empty spaces

Practice Lesson 5

Students should use the clock that is already drawn on the page to count out the minutes and hours for each problem.

Answer:1. 40 min.   4. 3:00 p.m.
2. 9:25 a.m.   5. 2:35 p.m.
3. 35 min.   6. 6:00 p.m.

Practice Lesson 6

This problem is solved by drawing a picture as in introductory lessons 1 and 2.

Answer: 18 cars, 2 motorcycles

Practice Lesson 7

This problem should begin by drawing a rectangle. Since the distance across the garden is 12 feet, students can label two sides 12 feet. This makes a total of 24 feet. That means the remaining two sides when added together are 40 feet; or 20 feet each.

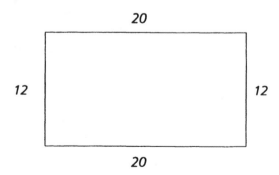

Answer: 12 feet by 20 feet

Practice Lesson 8

Students can draw 4 girls and for each girl draw 5 cupcakes. Then they can draw 5 boys and 6 cookies for each boy. Then they can count the total number of cupcakes and cookies.

Answer: 50 treats

Practice Lesson 9

Answer: 7 layers

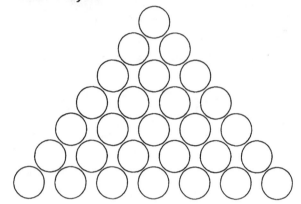

Name _____

Cats and Birds

Jan has pet cats and birds. She has 8 pets altogether. Her pets have a total of 24 legs. How many of her pets are birds?

Jan has _____ birds.

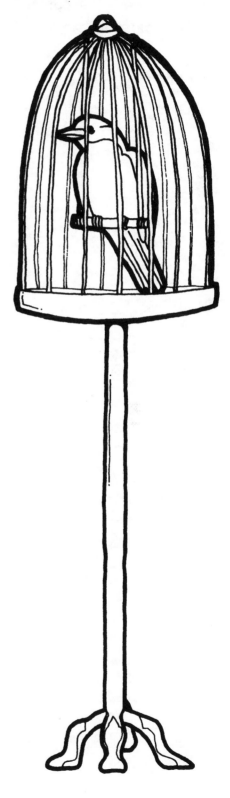

Name _____

Mary's Pets

Mary has hamsters, canaries and parrots. She has 6 pets altogether. If her pets have a total of 16 legs, how many of her pets are hamsters?

Mary has _____ hamsters.

Name _____

Tilt-a-Whirl Ride

The tilt-a-whirl at the carnival had 6 cars that each held 3 children. There were 25 children waiting to get on the ride when it stopped. Three children got into each of the 6 cars. How many were still waiting in line?

There were still _____ children waiting in line.

Name _____

Ferris Wheel

The ferris wheel has 8 chairs. Each chair has spaces for 3 people. If 10 people get on the ride, how many spaces will still be empty?

There will be _____ empty spaces.

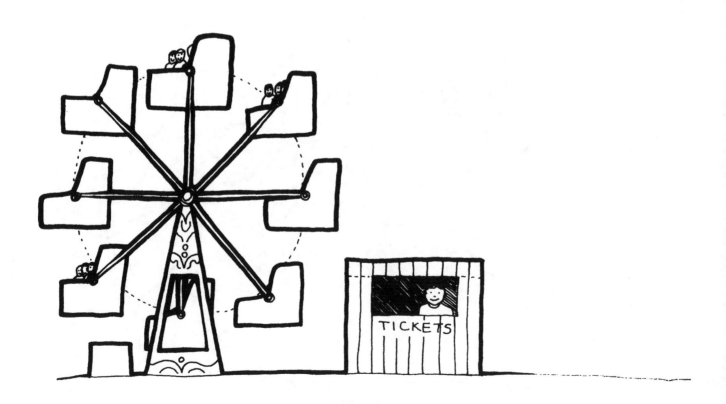

Name _____

School Time

Use the clock
to help you
figure out the
answers to
these problems.

1. Kim's lunch period at school starts at 11:45 a.m. and lasts until 12:25 p.m. How many minutes long is her lunch period? _____ minutes

2. Raul's math class starts at 8:40 a.m. The class is 45 minutes long. What time does it end? _____ a.m.

3. Tracy's gym class starts at 9:35 a.m. and ends at 10:10 a.m. How long is the gym class? _____ minutes

4. If the afternoon session begins at 12:25 p.m. and lasts 2 hours and 35 minutes, what time is school over? _____ p.m.

5. Yolanda gets out of school at 3:15 p.m. One day she left 40 minutes early for a doctor's appointment. What time did she leave? _____ p.m.

6. Pete got home from school at 3:35 p.m. He ate dinner 2 hours and 25 minutes later. What time did Pete eat dinner? _____ p.m.

Name _____

Sam's Used Wheels

Sam sells used vehicles. He has 20 cars and motorcycles on his lot. The vehicles have a total of 76 wheels. How many of his vehicles are cars? How many are motorcycles?

Sam has _____ cars and _____ motorcycles.

Name _____

Greta's Garden

When Greta walks around her garden she walks 64 feet. When she walks across her garden she walks 12 feet. How long and wide is her garden?

Greta's garden is _____ feet wide and _____ feet long.

Name _____

Party Treats

The Main Street families are having a party. Every girl is bringing 5 cupcakes. Every boy is bringing 6 cookies. Four girls and 5 boys are coming to the party. How many treats will they have at the party?

There will be _____ treats at the party.

Name _____

Cubby Holes

Room 4 uses round ice cream tubs for cubby holes. They stack them in a triangle. How many layers will they need in order to have enough cubby holes for 28 children?

There will be _____ layers.

Extend a Repeating Pattern

This strategy involves organizing information, looking for a pattern, and extending patterns to solve problems. The strategy of looking for patterns develops a child's ability to think logically. The ability to see patterns also facilitates the transfer of knowledge and allows the student to make predictions based on his/her observations.

The study of patterns is valuable to the pupil in the study of mathematics. Organizing information in a systematic way and then using the repetitive patterns to make predictions and solve problems will help students become more persistent and flexible problem solvers. Seeing patterns helps the student make sense of the known information.

Instructional Notes

Introductory Lesson 1

Students should complete the pattern by noting which fruit is eaten on each day. The calendar would look like this:

Sun	Mon	Tues	Wed	Thurs	Fri	Sat
			a	o	a	o
a	o	a	o	a	o	a
o	a	o	a	o	a	o
a	o	a	o	a	o	a

Answer: Thursday, apple

Introductory Lesson 2

Students should make a calendar as they did in lesson 1. In this problem, however, they will be charting 3 fruits — apple, orange, and then banana.

Sun	Mon	Tues	Wed	Thurs	Fri	Sat
	a	o	b	a	o	b
a	o	b	a	o	b	a
o	b	a	o	b	a	o
b	a	o	b	a	o	b

Answer: orange, Thursday

Introductory Lesson 3

Students should make a chart or list showing Bob's age and where he went each year for vacation. The sequence would look like this:

(5) Disney World
(6) beach
(7) camping
(8) Disney World
(9) beach
(10) camping
(11) Disney World
(12) beach

Answer: beach

Introductory Lesson 4

This lesson introduces a different kind of problem. In this case, students will have to analyze each sequence to determine what the rule is that generates the list of numbers. Then they can use the pattern to forecast the next three numbers.

Answer: 1. add 4 - 24, 28, 32
2. add 5, subtract 3 - 12, 9, 14
3. count by 1's, count by 5's - 5, 25, 6
4. subtract 3 - 12, 9, 6
5. double - 32, 64, 128

Practice Lesson 5

Students should make a list of the months of the year and then write the sequence of names to show who is feeding the dog each month. The sequence would look like this:

January - Matthew	July - Matthew
February - Sara	August - Sara
March - Jacob	September - Jacob
April - Matthew	October - Matthew
May - Sara	November - Sara
June - Jacob	December - Jacob

Answer: Matthew, Matthew

Practice Problem 6

3 - family, 4 - family, 5 - friends, 6 - family, 7 - family, 8 - friends, 9 - family, 10 - family, 11 - friends, 12 - family, 13 - family, 14 - friends, 15 - family, 16 - family, 17 - friends, 18 - family

Answer: 18 - family; 3 - family

Practice Problem 7

S	M	T	W	Th	F	S
		1		1		2
	1		1		1	
2		1				

Answer: Tuesday

Practice Problem 8

R	W	W	B	R
W	W	B	R	W
W	B	R	W	W
B	R	W	W	B
R	W	W	B	R

Answer: The 5th row repeats the pattern of the first row.

Practice Problem 9

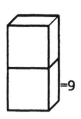

blocks	surface area
1	5
2	9
3	13
4	17
5	21
6	25

Answer: 25 squares

Practice Problem 10

T H		T	H	T	T H
	T	H	T	T H	
T	H	T	T H		T
	T	H	T H	T	
T					H

Answer: 5 times

Name _____

Apple or Orange?

Everyday Katie eats either an apple or an orange. She never eats the same fruit two days in a row. She eats an apple on the first Wednesday of the month. On what day will she eat the fifth apple? Which fruit will she eat on the fifth Wednesday?

Katie will eat the fifth apple on_____.

On the fifth Wednesday she will eat a_____.

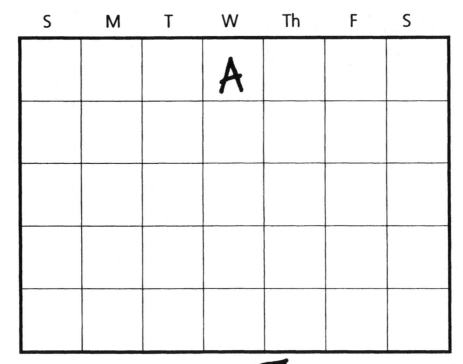

Name _____

A Fruity Problem

Kathy always eats an apple on one day, then an orange, and then a banana. What fruit will she eat on the second Monday? On what day of the week will she eat the sixth banana?

On the second Monday she will eat _____.

She will eat the sixth banana on _____.

Name _____

Vacation Plans

Each year Bob's family goes either camping, to Disney World, or to the beach (in that order). When Bob was 5 years old, they went to Disney World. Where will they go when Bob is 12 years old?

They will go to _____.

Name _____

Give Me Three

What are the next three numbers?

1. 4, 8, 12, 16, 20, _____, _____, _____

2. 1, 6, 3, 8, 5, 10, 7, _____, _____, _____

3. 1, 5, 2, 10, 3, 15, 4, 20, _____, _____, _____

4. 27, 24, 21, 18, 15, _____, _____, _____

5. 1, 2, 4, 8, 16, _____, _____, _____

Name _____

Feeding the Dog

Matthew, Sara and Jacob take turns feeding their dog. Each one does it for a month at a time. Matthew fed the dog in January, Sara fed the dog in February, and Jacob did it in March. Who will feed the dog in October? Who will feed the dog in January next year?

In October_____will feed the dog.

In January_____will feed the dog.

Name _____

Birthday Party

Every third year Colin has a birthday party with his friends. On the other years he has a family party. Colin had a party with his friends when he was 5 years old. What kind of party will he have when he is 18 years old? What kind of party did he have when he was 3 years old?

When he is 18 he will have a _____ party.

When he was 3 he had a _____ party.

Name _____

Baseball Schedule

The Cardinals baseball team will play ten baseball games in June. They will play every other day, starting on Tuesday. They play one game on weekdays and two games on Saturdays or Sundays. On what day of the week will their last game be played?

S	M	T	W	Th	F	S

Their last game was on_____.

Name _____

Color Blocks

How many rows do you color using the pattern red, white, white, blue before you have a row that is the same as the first row?

The pattern repeats on the _____ row.

Name _____

Painted Cubes

Carlos is stacking blocks and painting them. If he has only one block, he paints 5 squares. If he has two blocks, he paints 9 squares. How many squares will he paint when he has a tower of 6 blocks?

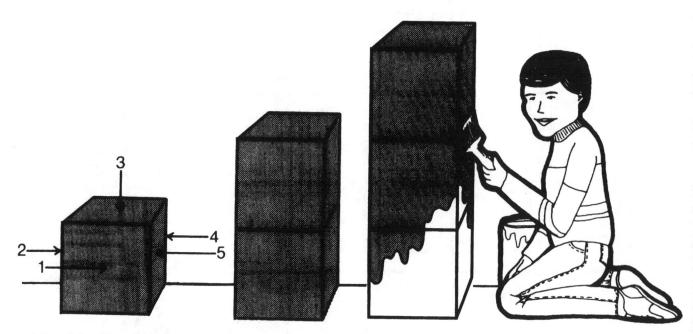

With 6 blocks, Carlos will paint _____ squares.

Name _____

Cool Dresser

Mr. Price wears a tie every other day. He wears his favorite Hawaiian shirt every third day. How many days during the month will he wear both his Hawaiian shirt and a tie?

Sun	Mon	Tues	Wed	Thurs	Fri	Sat
1 H. shirt tie	2	3	4	5	6	7
8	9	10	11	12	13	14
15	16	17	18	19	20	21
22	23	24	25	26	27	28
29	30					

Mr. Price wears his

Hawaiian shirt and

tie _____ times.

Make a Table or List

This strategy involves organizing data systematically to find solutions. Learning to make a table or an organized list will enable students to systematically account for all possibilities.

Recognizing patterns is an important skill young children should be encouraged to develop as they learn this strategy. As patterns emerge in the tables and lists they construct, students should be encouraged to look for, discuss, and use the patterns they see. Looking at the patterns that develop will also help students check their work. If there is a breakdown of the pattern somewhere in the table or list, they should look for an error in their work.

In this book we have included organized lists to account for all possibilities, such as the possible ages of Jack and Jill if the sum of their ages is 6:

Jack	Jill
1	5
2	4
3	3
4	2
5	1

We have also included tables and charts that refer to systematic organized lists like the following:

number of weeks	1	2	3	4
school days	5	10	15	20

Instructional Notes

Introductory Lesson 1
To solve this problem, students should make a table or list showing all the possible arrangements of pictures. They should start by making the arrangements with Molly's picture hanging on the left. Then they can list the possibilities with Jeff's picture and then Pete's picture on the left. The possible arrangements are:

M - J - P	M - P - J
J - P - M	J - M - P
P - J - M	P - M - J

Answer: 6 different arrangements

Introductory Lesson 2
This problem can be solved by making a table showing the days and the number of cans collected each day. The table would look like:

days	1	2	3	4	5	6	7
cans	5	10	15	20	25	30	35

Using the information in the table, students can easily find the answers to the questions.
Answer: 9 days, 35 cans

Introductory Lesson 3
This problems requires a table like the one constructed in lesson 2. Instead of 5 cans per day, students will complete the chart to show 3 dollars per day. They can then use the table to look up the answers to the questions.
Answer: 10 days, $39

Introductory Lesson 4
This problem can be solved by making a chart of all the possible combinations that when added together equal 18.
Answer:

Jenny	Dario
5	13
6	12
7	11
8	10
9	9
10	8
11	7
12	6
13	5

Introductory Lesson 5

This lesson should be completed by first making a table showing all the possible ages of the boys. Once the table has been constructed, students can locate the one set of ages that satisfies the second criterion that Carl be 2 years younger than Juan. The table for this problem would look like this:

possible ages

Carl	Juan
1	7
2	6
3	5
4	4
5	3
6	2
7	1

Answer: Carl - 3, Juan - 5

Practice Lesson 6

This problem is solved in a manner similar to lesson 5. First students will need to make a chart of all possible combinations. Then they can find the one combination that satisfies the criterion that Bill has 3 more pets than Lisa.

Possible number of pets are:

Lisa	Bill
1	6
2	5
3	4
5	2
6	1

Answer: Bill - 5, Lisa - 2

Practice Lesson 7

The different combinations are:

dolphin - forest - zoo
dolphin - zoo - forest
zoo - forest - dolphin
zoo - dolphin - forest
forest - zoo - dolphin
forest - dolphin - zoo

Answer: 6 possibilities

Practice Lesson 8

Reed and Marco's seats don't matter. The combinations for the other three people are:

Reed - Ann - Peter - Heidi - Marco
Reed - Ann - Heidi - Peter - Marco
Reed - Peter - Heidi - Ann - Marco
Reed - Peter - Ann - Heidi - Marco
Reed - Heidi - Peter - Ann - Marco
Reed - Heidi - Ann - Peter - Marco

Answer: 6 different ways

Practice Lesson 9

weeks	money
start	15
1	23
2	31
3	39
4	47

Answer: 4 weeks

Practice Lesson 10

flats	plants
1	12
2	24
3	36
4	48
5	60
6	72
7	84
8	96

Answer: 8 flats

Name _____

Hanging Pictures

Mrs. McGuire wanted to hang pictures of her three children (Molly, Jeff and Pete) in a row above her fireplace. How many different ways could she hang the pictures?

There are _____ different ways to arrange the pictures.

Name _____

Recycling Cans

Maria recycles 5 cans every day. How long will it take to collect 45 cans? How many cans will Maria have on the 7th day?

days	1	2	3	4	5	6	7	8	9	10
cans	5									

It takes _____ days to collect 45 cans.

In 7 days Maria collects _____ cans.

Name _____

Paper Route

Mark makes 3 dollars a day delivering newspapers. How long will it take Mark to make $30.00? How much money will he have earned on the 13th day?

days	1	2	3	4	5	6	7	8	9	10	11	12	13
dollars	3												

It takes Mark _____ days.

In 13 days he will have earned _____.

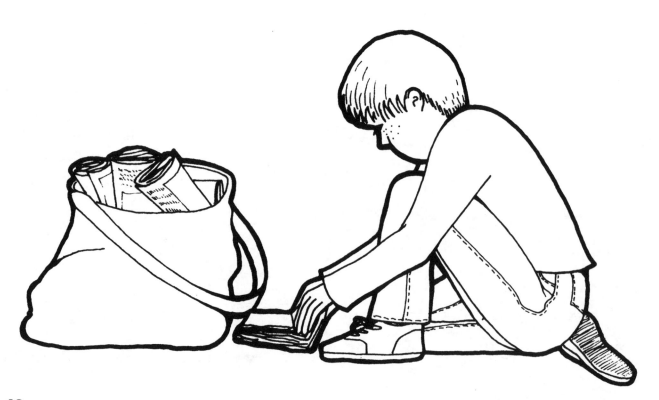

Name _____

Video Games

Jenny and Dario together have a total of 18 video games. Neither person has less than 5 games. What are all the possible numbers of games that Jenny and Dario could have?

Name _____

How Old?

Juan and Carl are neighbors. When their ages are added together the sum is 8. Carl is 2 years younger than Juan. How old are Juan and Carl?

Carl is _____ years old.

Juan is _____ years old.

Name _____

Pets

Bill and Lisa have 7 pets altogether. Bill has 3 more pets than Lisa. How many pets does each child have?

Bill has _____ pets, and Lisa has _____ pets.

Name _____

Zoo Plans

Curt's family is deciding in what order they will see the dolphin show, the tropical forest, and the petting zoo when they visit Sea World. How many different possibilities (different orders) are there for seeing all the attractions?

There are _____ different ways to see the attractions.

Name _____

Movie Seating

Heidi, Ann, Peter, Marco, and Reed went to the movie. They sat in the same row at the theater. Reed and Marco insisted on sitting in the end seats. How many different ways could the other three people be seated?

There are _____ different ways the people could be seated.

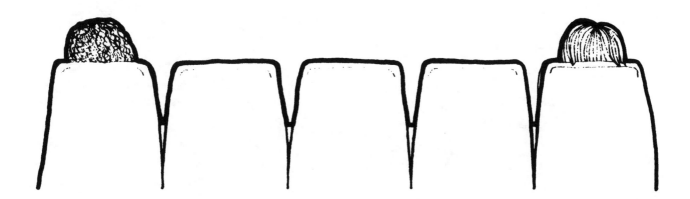

Name _____

Saving for Swimming

week	money
start	$15.00
1	$23.00
2	

Nancy wants to take swimming lessons. The lessons cost $47.00. She already has saved $15.00. If she saves $8.00 each week, how many weeks will it take until she has enough money for the lessons?

Nancy has to save for _____ weeks.

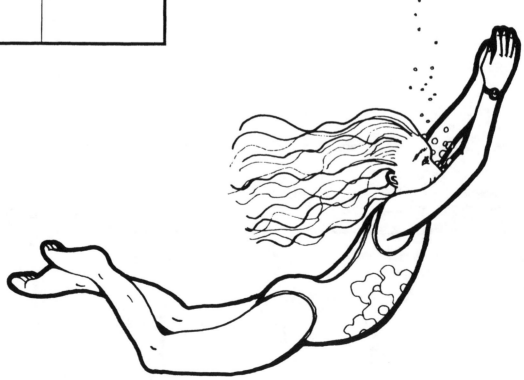

Name _____

Plants for Gifts

The second graders need 96 daisy plants for their Mother's Day gifts. Each flat contains 12 plants. How many flats does the class need for their gifts?

The class needs _____ flats of daisies.

flats	plants
1	12
2	

Choose Relevant Information

This strategy involves logical thinking about what the problem is asking and what information is needed in order to find the answer. Learning to choose relevant information for problem solving is essential if students are to become effective real-life problem solvers.

Thinking about the problem before attempting any answer should be encouraged in all problem solving. This involves understanding the problem, understanding the questions, finding the necessary information, and choosing the correct operation to solve the problem. Students should also be encouraged to think about their answers and to question whether they make sense. Estimation is an important skill that should be developed and encouraged as students check for sensible answers. Especially if students are using calculators to do computations, estimating and checking for reasonable answers are sensible habits to develop at an early age.

In this book we have used a variety of sources, such as charts, graphs, signs, recipes and time tables, that students need to refer to for the information needed to answer the questions. In real life, students will not be given two or three sentences with a couple of numbers in them that they will then add or subtract. Real life problems may not contain the key words "altogether," "more" or "less." Also in real life students may not always have the information they need to answer some questions. For this reason, we have included some problems that cannot be solved because there is missing information.

Steps for Analyzing Information and Solving Problems

The following steps will help students become better problem solvers.

1. Read the problem carefully.
2. Think about what the problem is asking.
3. Decide what information is needed in order to answer the question.
4. Think about where you can get this information. If you have too much information, disregard unimportant information.
5. Decide how you will solve the problem.
6. Do the computations.
7. Think about your answer. Does it make sense? Does it answer the question?

Instructional Notes

Introductory Lesson 1

Students should first read the question and think about what the problem is asking and what information is needed. It would be helpful if students circled the needed information in the drawings. They should circle the information for each question in a different color. For instance, they could circle the information for the first question in red, the information for the second question in blue, and the information for the third question in green. Once they have located this information, they can then proceed to do the computations.

Answer:
1. 75¢
2. $30.00
3. Luis - $4.35
   David - $18.40
   difference $14.05

Introductory Lesson 2

Sometimes when students try to solve a problem they discover that they don't have all the information they need. If they do not have all of the relevant information, they cannot solve the problem. Read each situation with students. Together decide what information is missing.

Answer:
1. what time they started painting
2. how long it takes to drive to Uncle Larry's house
3. what coins they have and, therefore, how much money they have
4. how much ribbon is on each roll

Practice Lessons 3 - 5

In these lessons students should locate the information in the pictures, chart and graph. While most questions call for the interpretation of the given information or simple computations using the given information, some questions cannot be answered because there is not enough information.

Practice Lesson 3

Answer:
1. 40¢
2. yes, total would be 90¢
3. 3 pencils - 1 eraser, 1 pencil - 5 erasers, 2 pencils - 3 erasers, 0 pencils - 7 erasers
4. M.I.
5. A pad of paper and crayons cost 75¢; with the remaining 15¢ she could buy 1 pencil and 1 eraser or 3 erasers
6. M.I.

Practice Lesson 4

Answer:
1. 7   3. 11
2. 31   4. M.I.

Practice Lesson 5

Answer:
1. 8
2. M.I.
3. 2
4. 10
5. blue, purple, red, black, green, orange, yellow

Name _____

Shopping

1. Joanne bought a bag of jelly beans, a lollipop, and a candy bar. How much money did she spend? _____

2. Steve bought a new bat, a ball and a glove. How much did Steve's purchases cost? _____

3. Mrs. Gonzales took her sons shopping. Luis bought a poster, jelly beans and a lollipop. David bought baseball shoes and a candy bar. How much more than Luis did David spend? _____

Name _____

Missing Parts

Read each problem. Tell what information is missing.

1. Tony and Todd were painting the fence. They figured it would take 3 hours to paint the fence. Did they finish in time to go to their baseball game at 4:00 p.m.?

   missing information _____

2. D.J. and Curt are invited to their Uncle Larry's for dinner at 6:00 p.m. Will they arrive on time if they leave home at 5:30 p.m.?

   missing information _____

3. Terri and Melissa had 8 coins between them. A single dip ice cream cone cost 50¢ and a double dip cone cost 75¢. Did they have enough money to buy the single dip cone for Terri and a double dip for Melissa?

   missing information _____

4. Linda has 12 Christmas presents to wrap. She needs 5 feet of ribbon for each package. She bought two rolls of ribbon. How much ribbon will she have left over after she wraps all of the presents?

   missing information _____

Name _____

School Store

Use the information in the pictures to solve the problems. If you cannot solve the problem because there is not enough information, write M.I. (for missing information) on the line.

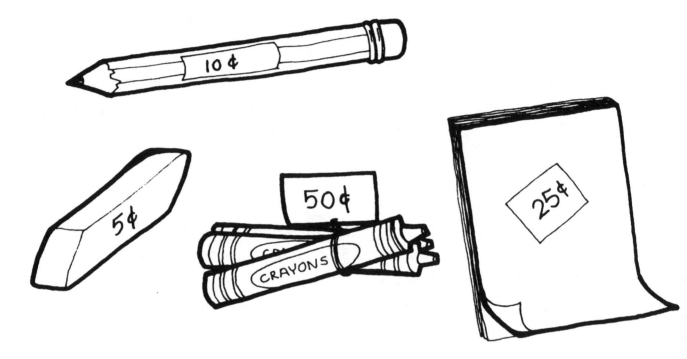

1. How much does a pencil, eraser and paper cost? _____

2. If you bought one of each item, would a dollar be enough to pay for your purchases? _____

3. What possible combinations of pencils and erasers could you buy with 35¢?

   _____ pencils and _____ erasers   _____ pencils and _____ erasers

   _____ pencils and _____ erasers   _____ pencils and _____ erasers

4. If Sean bought a pencil and an eraser for each of the people coming to his birthday party, how much would it cost? _____

5. Amy had 90¢ to spend. She bought a pad of paper and a box of crayons. What could she buy with the remaining money?_____

6. If Matt bought a box of crayons, 3 pencils, and an eraser, how much change would he receive? _____

Name _____

Class Pets

Room 4 made a graph showing their pets. Use the chart to answer the following questions. If you cannot answer the question because there is not enough information given, write M.I. (for missing information) on the line.

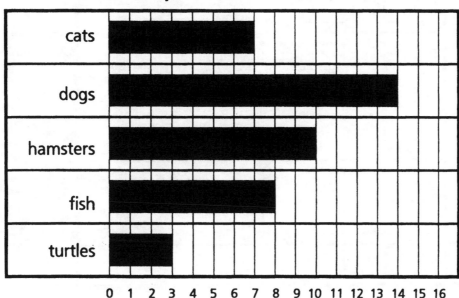

Class Pets Graph

1. How many more dogs are there than cats? _____

2. How many pets are mammals? _____

3. How many pets are either fish or turtles? _____

4. How many students have both a dog and a cat? _____

Name _____

Favorite Colors

The third grade made a graph of their favorite colors. Use the chart to answer the following questions. If you cannot answer the question because there is not enough information given, write M.I. (for missing information) on the line.

Third Grade Favorite Color Graph

red	☐☐☐☐☐
blue	☐☐☐☐☐☐☐☐☐☐☐
orange	☐☐☐
yellow	☐☐
black	☐☐☐☐◸
purple	☐☐☐☐☐☐
green	☐☐☐◸

☐ = 2 children

1. How many more children chose purple than chose yellow? _____

2. How many more boys than girls chose black? _____

3. How many more children chose blue than chose red, orange and yellow together? _____

4. How many fewer children chose purple than chose blue? _____

5. List the favorite colors from most favorite to least favorite.

1._____ 2._____ 3._____

4._____ 5._____ 6._____

7._____

Application Problems

The problems in this section of the book are to be used to practice the five strategies that have been presented in the first half of this book. The strategies are not indicated on the problems, because students should be free to try several different strategies. There is never just one way to solve a problem. One student may find the correct answer by using one strategy while another student may be successful using another strategy. Encourage students to play around with the problems and to persevere until they find a strategy that works.

While several strategies can be used to solve most problems, you may want to select additional problems to reinforce or give additional work on a particular strategy. In this case, the following list of problems that can be used for a particular strategy could be helpful.

Use manipulatives or act out
Use practice problems
3, 4, 7, 10, 19, 20, 21, 22, 24, 25, 29, 30, 34, 40, 42, 49, 50

Draw a picture or diagram
Use practice problems
1, 2, 8, 9, 36, 41, 43, 44

Extend a pattern
Use practice problems
5, 6, 11, 12, 23, 33, 35, 37, 38, 45, 46

Make a table or list
Use practice problems
13, 14, 15, 16, 17, 18, 26, 27, 28, 31, 32, 39, 47, 48

Choose relevant information
Use practice problems
51, 52, 53, 54, 55

The problems in this section are printed two per page. One way to use these problems is to cut the pages in half and duplicate one problem at the top of an 8 1/2" by 11 " piece of paper, thus giving students the bottom half of the sheet of paper to work the problem and record their answers. You can also use them to make a set of math task cards that can be used in a learning center or for enrichment. Another use is to give one problem to each cooperative learning group, instructing them to record their work on another piece of paper.

Name _____

Grand Opening

At the grand opening of the Big Burger restaurant, customers received balloons. Every fourth customer received a gold balloon that entitled them to a free hamburger. If 39 balloons were given out, how many received gold balloons?

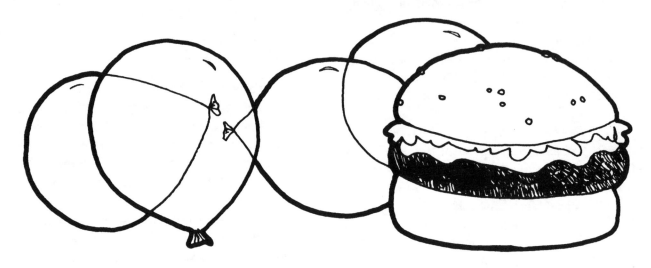

Name _____

School Bus

The school bus has seven rows of seats on each side of the aisle. Only two people can sit in each of the front seats and only two people can sit in each of the back seats. Three people can sit in other seats. How many children can ride the bus?

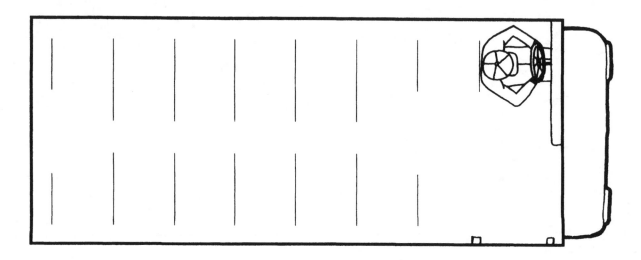

Name _____

Loose Change

Jack has 2 quarters and 2 dimes. Jeannie has 1 quarter, 2 dimes, and 1 nickel. How much money would Jack have to give Jeannie so that they have the same amount?

Name _____

Valentines

Jim, Heather, Greg, and Kristy each made valentines. They made 28 cards altogether. Each person made at least 4 valentines. Jim made twice as many as Heather. Greg made 2 more than Heather. Kristy made 2 more than Jim. How many valentines did each person make?

Name _____

Car Pool

Sara and Rita's mothers take turns driving the girls to school. Each mother drives 3 days in a row. Sara's mother drove the first 3 days (Monday, Tuesday, Wednesday). Rita's mother drove the next three school days (Thursday, Friday, Monday). How many days did Rita's mother drive in a four-week period?

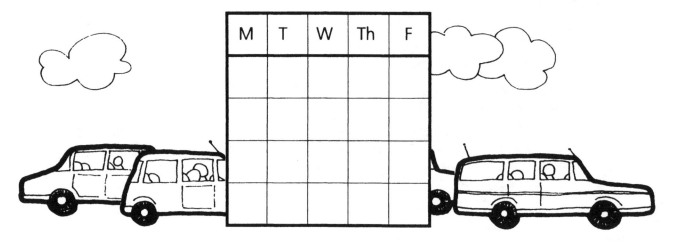

Name _____

Quilt Squares?

You are making a quilt that has five rows of five squares per row. You have 15 white squares, 10 red squares and 10 blue squares. You have more squares than you will need to make the quilt. What are two different repeating patterns you could use to arrange the squares? How many of each color will you have left over?

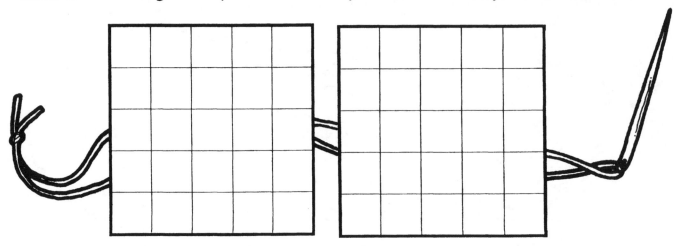

Name _____

Moving Chairs

Carlos and Charlie had to carry 36 chairs to the gym. How many trips would they have to make if Charlie carried 4 chairs at a time and Carlos carried 2 chairs at a time?

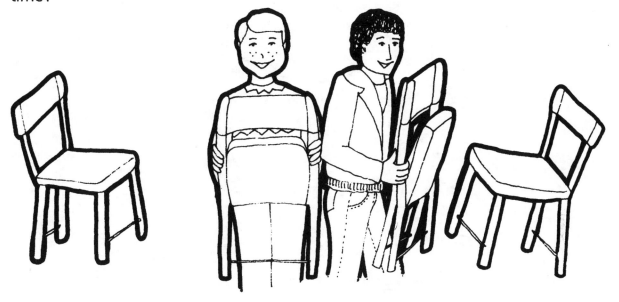

Name _____

Hot Dogs

The 20 students in Mrs. Galvin's class decided to have a hot dog lunch. If 9 of the students ordered 3 hot dogs each and the other students ordered 2 hot dogs each, how many hot dogs did Mrs. Galvin have to buy?

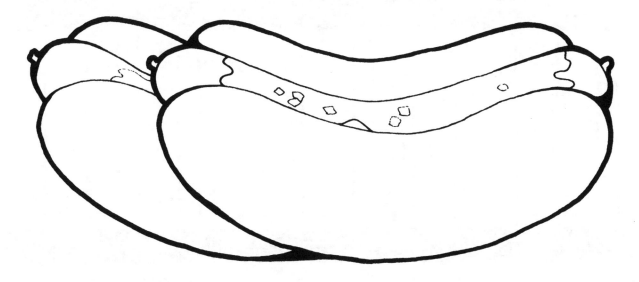

Name _____

Frogs in a Pond

There are 10 lily pads in the pond. The two largest pads can hold 3 frogs. The other pads can hold 2 frogs. If 34 frogs jump into the pond, how many frogs will not be able to sit on a lily pad?

Name _____

Library Books

Ms. Riggs had 20 library books about pets on a shelf. Tina checked out 4 of the books. Her teacher returned 5 books and checked out 8 new books for the class. How many books were on the shelf then?

Name _____

Paper Chains

The second graders in Riley School were decorating their classroom. They made a paper chain using this pattern — pink, pink, yellow, pink, green, green, blue. If they repeated this pattern 5 times, how many strips of each color would they need? How many strips altogether would they need to make this chain?

Name _____

Squares

Continue the pattern below. What will the sixth square look like?

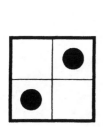 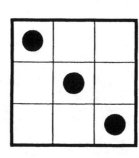 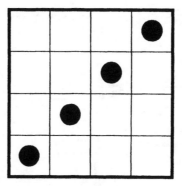

Name _____

Attendance Helpers

Mrs. Murphy chose a boy to take the attendance to the office one day and a girl the next day. She started the school year with a boy and continued taking turns. Did a boy or girl take the attendance on the 10th day? Who took the attendance on the 100th day?

Name _____

Measuring Sugar

Cathy Cook has a 2-cup measuring cup and a 1-cup measuring cup. She needs to measure 6 cups of sugar. How many different ways can she measure six cups?

Name _____

Comparing Ages

Todd is three years older than Cammie. If their ages added together equal 13, how old is Todd? How old is Cammie?

Name _____

Pieces of Pizza

George and Paul split a medium pizza that had been cut into 12 pieces. If George ate twice as many pieces as Paul, how many pieces did each boy eat?

Name _____

Miniature Collection

For his birthday Tony got 10 miniature cars and trucks. He got 2 more cars than trucks. How many trucks did he get? How many cars did he get?

Name _____

Teddy Bears

Anna and Megan collect teddy bears. Each girl has more than 5 bears in her collection. Together the girls have 18 teddy bears. How many teddy bears might each girl have? Find all the possible answers.

Name _____

Books to Share

Donnie, Ed and Betty brought a total of 24 animal books to school to share with their class. Donnie brought 2 more than Ed. Betty brought 2 more than Donnie. How many animal books did each person bring?

Name _____

Sticker Stickler

Maggie had 16 stickers and Hank had 12 stickers. They each used 8 of their stickers. After they had used these stickers, how many stickers would Maggie have to give Hank so they would each have the same number of stickers?

Name _____

The Line Up

Bob, Carmen, Marco, Steve, Diane and Raul lined up from shortest to tallest. Bob stood behind Carmen and in front of Diane. Marco stood behind Raul and in front of Steve. Carmen was the shortest person in the line. Who was the tallest? Who was the fourth person in line?

Name _____

The Car Race

Five cars (blue, red, orange, green, and yellow) finished a race. The red car came in third, before the green car. The yellow car finished just ahead of the blue car. The blue car was not last. Which car won the race?

Name _____

Watering Plants

Alexis, Karen and Charlie took turns watering the flowers for eleven weeks during the summer. Karen watered the flowers the first week, Charlie did it the second week, and Alexis the third. If they continued in this order, who was the last one to water the flowers?

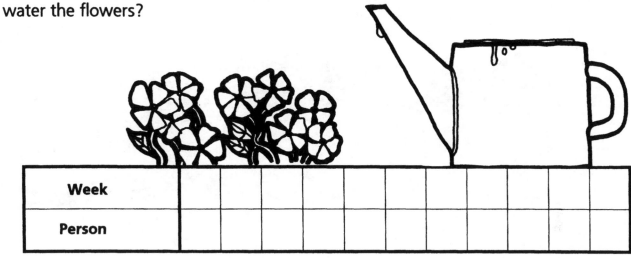

Week										
Person										

Stacked Books

How can you put 21 books in three stacks so that there are twice as many books in the second stack as in the first stack and the third stack has twice as many books as the second stack?

Name _____

Bug Collection

Eric is counting the legs on his bug collection. His spiders have 8 legs. His beetles and crickets have 6 legs each. He counts a total of 48 legs. He has a total of 7 bugs. How many spiders does he have? How many beetles and crickets does he have?

Name _____

Flower Shop Figuring

In the flower shop there are red flower pots that hold three flowers each. How many flower pots would Theresa need to plant 15 flowers? How many flowers would fit in 7 pots?

Name _____

Cake Bake

The royal baker had to bake 32 cakes for the king and queen's party. By Wednesday he had baked 24 cakes. If he baked two cakes every day after that, on what day did he finish?

Name _____

Jeans Money

Barbara earns $5.00 each week by doing chores. She has $9.00 in her bank already. How many weeks will she have to work to buy a pair of jeans that cost $25.00?

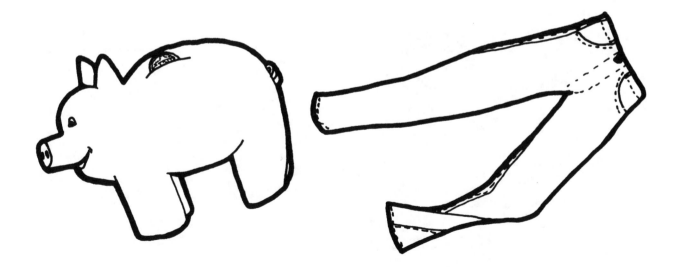

Name _____

Sally's Designs

Sally made a geometric design using 10 rectangles and triangles. The shapes she used in her design had 36 corners altogether. How many of the shapes were triangles?

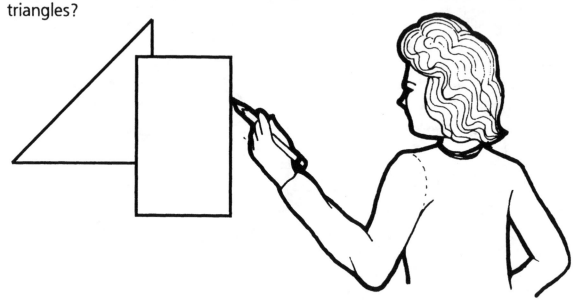

Name _____

Triangles in the Square

John made a design using triangles inside of squares. Inside each square there were one red triangle, one blue triangle, one green triangle, and one yellow triangle. If there were 20 triangles in his design, how many squares did he use?

Name _____

Comparing Cousins

Chin has an older cousin, Lee. When their ages are added together they equal 20. If Chin is at least 6 years old, what are all the possible ages the boys could be?

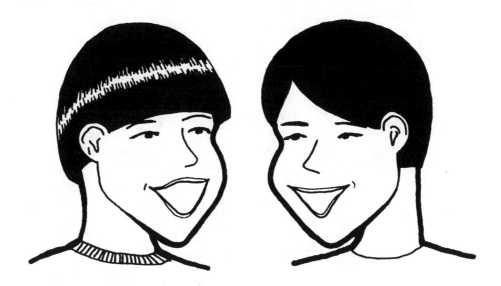

Name _____

Baseball Cards

Tony and Tasha have collected baseball cards for a long time. Tasha has 2 more albums of cards than Tony. Together they have 16 albums. How many albums does each one have?

Name _____

Winner or Loser?

You are playing a game. You start with 25 points. On your first turn (and every odd turn after that) you win 10 points. On your second turn (and every even turn after that) you lose 3 points. How many points do you have after your 8th turn?

Name _____

Field Trip

Twenty - four (24) children in the preschool are going on a field trip to the zoo. For every 8 children there will be 1 teacher. There will also be 1 parent for every 4 children. How many parents and how many teachers will be going on the field trip?

Name _____

Red, White and Blue Afghan

Mrs. Santiago is knitting an afghan. It is made of
six rows with 5 squares in each row. She is using
the pattern red - blue - white - red - blue - white. If
she continues this pattern for the whole afgan
what color will the last square be?

Name _____

Car Race

There are 12 cars that finished the Indianapolis 500 race. Four cars finished ahead
of the red race car. How many finished after the red race car?

Name _____

Flag Duty

The 4th, 5th and 6th graders at Southside School took turns each month putting up the flag. The 6th grade started out in September, the 5th grade did it in October, and the 4th grade did it in November. They continued this pattern all year. Who put the flag up in June?

Name _____

Flower Garden

Mr. Chong planted his garden in 5 rows with 5 flowers in each row. He planted the flowers in a repeating pattern of red - yellow - white. If he repeated that pattern, which color did he use most in the garden?

Name _____

Arcade Fun

When Jose plays video games at the arcade he gets 1 ticket for every 8 points he scores. How many points does Jose need to score in order to get 4 tickets? If Jose scored 48 points, how many tickets would he get?

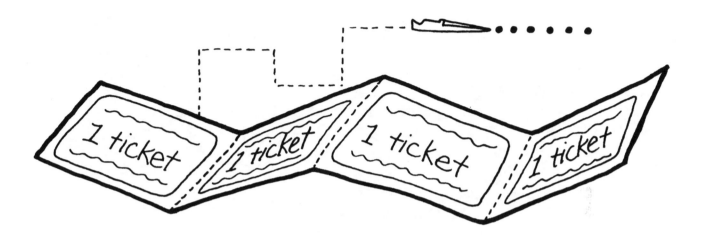

Name _____

Standing in Line

The baseball tickets at the stadium were going on sale at 4:00 p.m. At 1:00 p.m. 15 people were in line waiting to buy tickets. Every 15 minutes 10 more people got in line. At what time were there 85 people in line? How many people were in line at 2:15 p.m.?

Name _____

Carnival Booths

Briar Glen School needed workers for its carnival. The ring toss, darts, and bottle game each needed 2 workers. The fishing and basketball booths each needed 3 workers. The cake walk, frisbee toss, and relay each needed 4 workers. How many workers would be needed to run the 8 game booths?

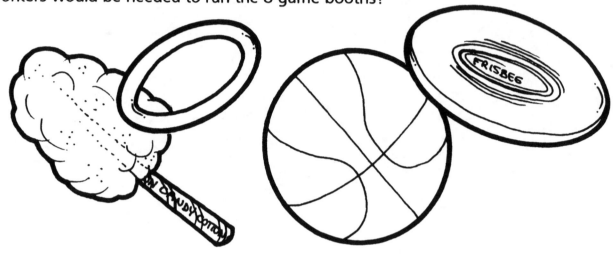

Name _____

Play Money

Elizabeth was the banker for the game "Buy and Sell." She distributed the play money. Each player got the following amounts:

$100 bills -   4 each
$50 bills -   4 each
$10 bills - 10 each
$5 bills - 10 each

How many bills did she distribute if there were 4 players? How much money did each player get?

Name _____

Fence Building

Mr. Park put a fence up across the front of his yard. First he dug 10 holes for the 10 fence posts. He put the fence posts 3 meters apart. How many meters long was his fence?

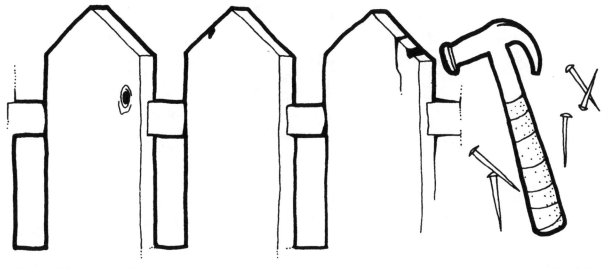

Name _____

Cake Decorating

Lola began decorating cakes at 8:00 a.m. It takes her 2 hours to decorate each cake. She takes a one-hour lunch break after she finishes the second cake. What time will she finish decorating the third cake? Will she have time to decorate a fourth cake before dinner at 5:30 p.m.?

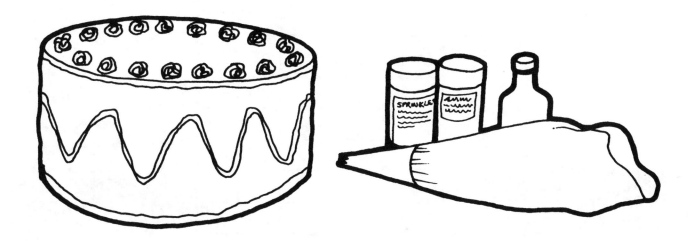

Name _____

Vacationing with Grandpa

Grandpa takes one of his three grandchildren on a trip with him each year. Robby went in 1992. In 1991, his cousin Susan went on the trip. His brother Matthew went in 1993. If Grandpa continues this pattern, who will go with him in the year 2000?

Name _____

Watering the Lawn

Mrs. Garcia lived in a town where she could only water her grass on even-numbered days of the month. She watered her lawn on Tuesday, June 2nd. How many times in June was she able to water her lawn on a Saturday? What day of the week had the most even-numbered dates when she could water?

June						
S	M	T	W	Th	F	S

Name _____

Making Address Books

Mrs. Fugi's scout troop was going to make address books for their mothers. For every book they would need 10 sheets of paper. How many sheets of paper would be needed for 6 children to make the address book? How much paper for 12 children?

Name _____

Pom Poms

The cheerleaders are buying new pom poms. If each set of pom poms cost $11.00, how much will it cost to buy 6 sets? If they have already raised $50.00, how much more money do they need?

Name _____

Making Cookies

Aunt Irma was making smiley face cookies. For each cookie she used:

2 life savers for the eyes

4 raisins for the mouth

1 chocolate chip for the nose

How many cookies could she make if she had:

24 life savers

40 raisins

15 chocolate chips

What ingredients would she have left?

Name _____

Going to the Zoo

Thirty-one (31) people were traveling to the zoo in cars and vans. Each van held 8 people. Each car held 5 people. If 2 of the vehicles were vans, how many cars were needed to carry the rest of the people?

Name _____

School Cafeteria

potato chips 25¢	apple 10¢	hamburger 75¢
milk 15¢	pizza 50¢	banana 5¢

Use these prices to answer the questions. If the information you need to solve the problem is not given, write M.I. (for missing information) on the line.

1. How much money would you need to buy 2 pieces of pizza and a glass of milk?
   _____

2. What two different items could you buy for exactly $1.00? _____

3. If Mark has $3.00, how many pieces of pizza could he buy for himself and his friends?_____

4. If Alex has $1.20 and he buys a hamburger, how many glasses of milk could he buy with the remaining money?_____

5. If Gina had $1.25 and she bought potato chips for each of the friends she was eating lunch with, how much money would she have left?_____

6. How much would it cost Buster to buy 3 bags of potato chips, an apple and a banana?_____

7. How much more does a hamburger cost than a piece of pizza?_____

8. If Grace has a hamburger, a piece of fruit, and a glass of milk for her lunch, how much change would she get back from $1.00?_____

Name _____

Now You're Cooking

Caramel Popcorn	**Fruit Punch**
3 quarts popped corn	1 12-ounce can apricot juice
2 cups salted peanuts	1 12-ounce can orange juice
1 cup granulated sugar	1 12-ounce can pineapple juice
1 cup hot water	2 cups ginger ale
1/2 cup brown sugar	

Use the recipes above to answer the questions below. If you cannot answer a question because the information you need is not given, write M.I. (for missing information) on the line.

1. If you doubled the recipe for caramel popcorn, how much of each ingredient would you need?

    _____popped corn  _____salted peanuts

    _____granulated sugar _____hot water

    _____brown sugar

2. Altogether, how many ounces of fruit juices would you put into one batch of fruit punch? _____

3. Since there are 8 ounces in a cup, how many ounces of ginger ale would you put in for the fruit punch? _____

4. How many more ounces of ginger ale than apricot juice would you put in one batch? _____

5. If you wanted to make enough caramel popcorn for 30 people, how many batches of the recipe would you need to make? _____

Name _____

Basketball Scores

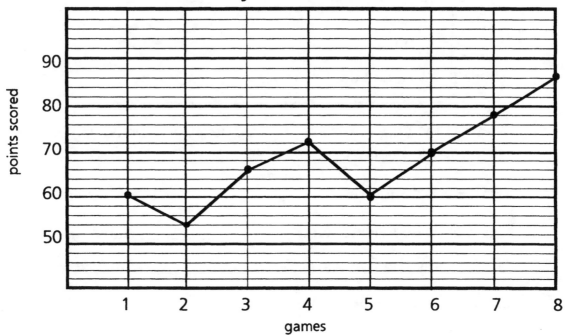

Points scored by Lincoln Lions Basketball Team

1. In what two games did the Lions score 60 points? _____ _____

2. How many more points did they score in game 4 than they scored in game 3?
_____

3. How many more points did they score in their highest scoring game than they scored in their lowest scoring game? _____

4. If the Lions scored 92 points in a tournament play-off game, how many more points was that than their highest regular season game? _____

Problem Solving Application

Name _____

Puppet Theater

See Your Favorite Fairy Tales

Adults - $1.50   Children 50¢

Saturday Show Times:

Little Red Riding Hood	1:00 - 2:00
Hansel and Gretel	2:30 - 3:45
Beauty and the Beast	4:30 - 5:20
Cinderella	6:00 - 7:05
Jack and the Beanstalk	7:30 - 8:25

1. If you arrived at the puppet theater at 12:30, how long would you have to wait for the first show to begin? _____

2. How long does each show last?

   _____ Little Red Riding Hood   _____Hansel and Gretel

   _____Beauty and the Beast   _____Cinderella

   _____Jack and the Beanstalk

3. Which show is the longest? _____

4. Which show is the shortest? _____

5. How much shorter is Cinderella than Hansel and Gretel?_____

6. If three children and two adults went to the show, how much would their tickets cost?_____

7. How much more would it cost for 6 adults than for 6 children to go to the puppet show?_____

© Prufrock Press Inc • *Primarily Math*

Name _____

Selling Subscriptions

The band at Glen Crest School sold magazines to raise money for a band trip. The graphs below show the sales of the winning team. Use the graphs to answer the questions below.

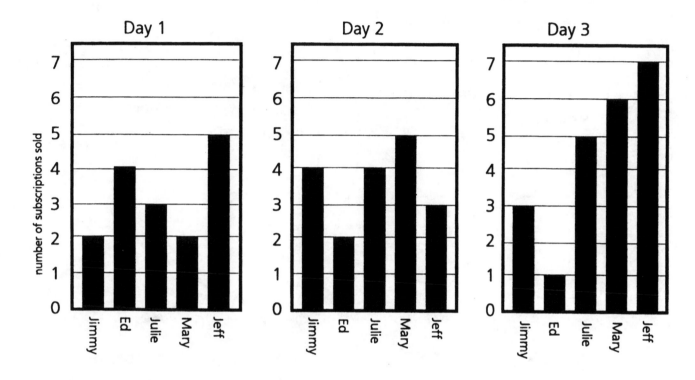

1. How many more subscriptions did Mary sell on day 3 than she sold on day 1?
   _____

2. How many subscriptions did Julie sell in all 3 days?_____

3. How many subscriptions did Ed sell in all 3 days?_____

4. How many more subscriptions did Julie sell in the contest than Ed?_____

5. Who sold the most magazines? _____
   How many subscriptions did that person sell altogether?_____

6. On which day did the team sell the most subscriptions?_____

Problem Solving Step - by - Step

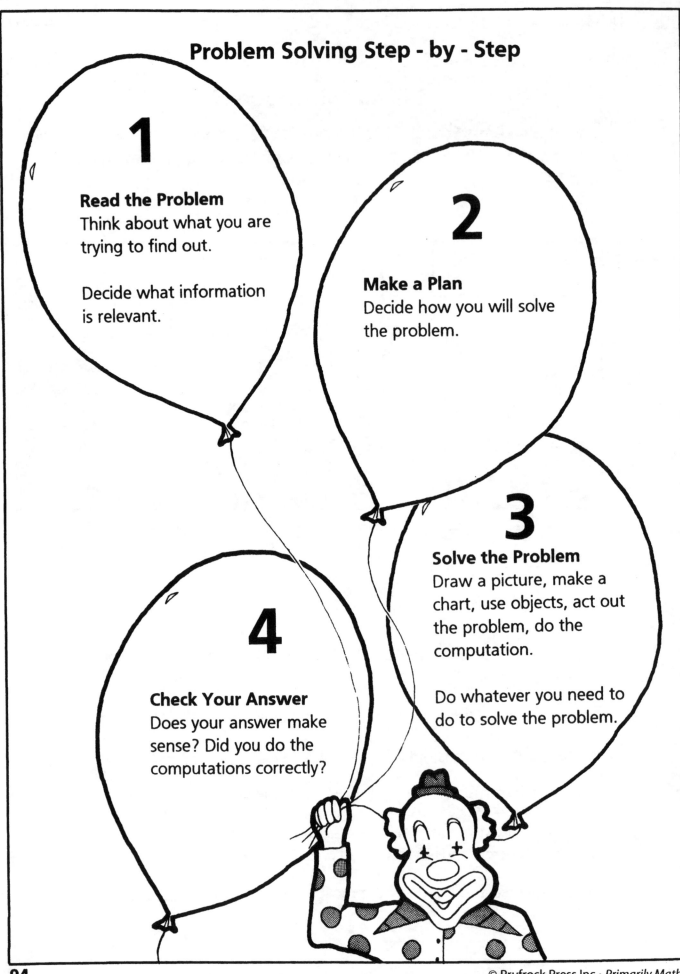

1

Read the Problem
Think about what you are trying to find out.

Decide what information is relevant.

2

Make a Plan
Decide how you will solve the problem.

3

Solve the Problem
Draw a picture, make a chart, use objects, act out the problem, do the computation.

Do whatever you need to do to solve the problem.

4

Check Your Answer
Does your answer make sense? Did you do the computations correctly?

Answers

Problem 1
9 gold balloons

Problem 2
38 children

Problem 3
Jack should give Jeannie 10¢
(1 dime).

Problem 4
Jim - 8   Greg - 6
Heather - 4 Kristy - 10

Problem 5
Rita's mother drove 9 times.

Problem 6
Several answers posible.
See examples, next page.

Problem 7
6 trips

Problem 8
49 hot dogs

Problem 9
12 frogs will not be on lily pads.

Problem 10
13 books on the shelf.

Problem 11
15 pink   10 green
5 yellow   5 blue
35 altogether

Problem 12
7 x 7 square

Problem 13
10th day - girl
100th day - girl

Problem 14

2 cup	1 cup
0	6
1	4
2	2
3	0

Problem 15
Todd - 8, Cammie - 5

Problem 16
George - 8, Paul - 4

Problem 17
cars - 6, trucks - 4

Problem 18

Anna	Megan
5	13
6	12
7	11
8	10
9	9
10	8
11	7
12	6
13	5

Problem 19
Ed - 6, Betty - 10, Donnie 8

Problem 20
Maggie would give Hank 2
stickers so they would each have
6 stickers.

Problem 21
Carmen, Bob, Diane, Raul,
Marco, Steve
Steve was the tallest, Raul was
fourth in line.

Problem 22
yellow, blue, red, green, orange
yellow car won.

Problem 23
Charlie

Problem 24
1st - 3 books, 2nd - 6 books,
3rd - 12 books

Problem 25
3 spiders, 4 beetles and crickets

Problem 26
5 pots, 21 flowers

Problem 27
Sunday

Problem 28
In four weeks she will have
$29.00.

Problem 29
6 rectangles, 4 triangles

Problem 30
5 squares

Problem 31

Chin	Lee
6	14
7	13
8	12
9	11

Problem 32
Tasha - 9 albums, Tony - 7 albums

Problem 33
53 points

Problem 34
6 parents and 3 teachers

Problem 35
white

Problem 36
7 cars

Problem 37
6th grade

Problem 38
red

Problem 39
4 tickets - 32 points,
6 tickets - 48 points

Problem 40
85 people at 2:45, 65 people at
2:15

Problem 41
24 workers

Problem 42
112 bills; $750.00 each

Problem 43
27 meters

Problem 44
3:00 p.m., yes

Problem 45
Susan

Problem 46

twice (the 6th and 20th); Tuesday

Problem 47

60 sheets, 120 sheets

Problem 48

$66.00; $16.00

Problem 49

10 cookies;
leftovers - 4 lifesavers, 0 raisins,
5 chocolate chips

Problem 50

3 cars

Problem 51

1. $1.15
2. chips and hamburger
3. 6 pieces
4. 3 glasses of milk
5. MI
6. 90¢
7. 25¢
8. MI

Problem 52

1. popped corn - 6 quarts
   granulated sugar - 2 cups
   brown sugar - 1 cup
   peanuts - 4 cups
   water - 2 cups
2. 36 ounces
3. 16 ounces
4. 4 ounces
5. MI

Problem 53

1. games 1 and 5
2. 6 points
3. 32 points
4. 6 points

Problem 54

1. 30 minutes
2. Riding Hood - 1 hour
   Beast - 50 minutes
   Beanstalk - 55 minutes
   Gretel - 1 hour 15 minutes
   Cinderella - 1 hour 5 minutes
3. Hansel and Gretel
4. Beauty and the Beast
5. 10 minutes
6. $4.50
7. $6.00

Problem 55

1. 4 subscriptions
2. 12 subscriptions
3. 7 subscriptions
4. 5 subscriptions
5. Jeff, 15 subscriptions
6. day 3

Problem 6

Some possible arrangements would be:

r w b r w	w r w b w	r b w w r	w b r w b
b r w b r	r w b w r	b w w r b	r w b r w
w b r w b	w b w r w	w w r b w	b r w b r
r w b r w	b w r w b	w r b w w	w r b w b
b r w b r	w r w b w	r b w w r	r w b r w

left overs:

r - 1	r - 4	r - 3	r - 2
w - 7	w - 2	w - 3	w - 6
b - 2	b - 4	b - 4	b - 2